78 and Counting!

Lockdown Living

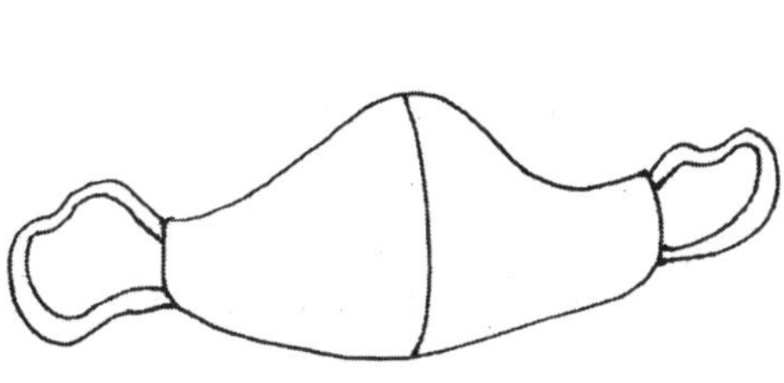

Joyce

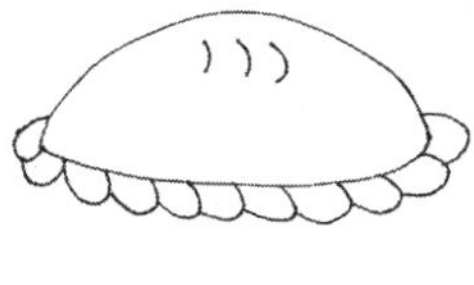

First published in Great Britain in 2020.

Cover illustrations by Joyce.

A CIP catalogue record for this book is
available from the British Library.

ISBN: 978-0-9928417-2-0

Printed and bound by ImprintDigital.com.

A huge thank you to all of my dear family and to my lovely friends who have continually encouraged and inspired me to write my rhymes and to even dare publish them!

Joyce x

CONTENTS

July 2020

August 2020

September 2020

Lockdown Living

I'm 79!

And now I've reached aged 79
and what a year it's been,
For who could have imagined pandemic C19?
And even now it's six months on
the world is still askew
And when it will come right again
we still don't have a clue.

But through the suffering
some good things have risen to the fore.
We're valuing our planet
and the natural world much more.
And we've been given time
to re-evaluate our lives,
Take pleasure in the simple things,
slow down … and we've survived
By doing things like gardening
and learning how to cook
And DIY and making things … and me?

I WROTE TWO BOOKS!

MARCH 2020

Our World

Could this terrible thing be doing some good
To this Earth where we live? If only we could
Learn a lesson from this.
How much we pollute
With our industry, air travel, daily commute!
Venice is CLEAN, its canals running clear.
Our carbon emissions are lowest this year!
50% reduced rate in New York!
We simply MUST sit round the table
and TALK!
Look at the big picture and surely take note.
LOOK, LISTEN and LEARN
is what gets MY vote.
If all our world's scientists gather as one
Then saving our world has surely begun!

The First Day Of Spring

It's the first day of spring,
so open your windows
And take a deep breath of fresh air!
There's little pollution so here's a solution
When weighed down with worry and care.
Just fill up your lungs and burst into song.
It'll be such a positive thing.
Just let it all out. (But don't scream or shout.)
Choose your favourite song and just SING!
We're all feeling blue … at a loss what to do.
We don't know what the future may bring.
Just sing and be jolly.
You won't need your brolly
And you might find the neighbours join in!

Isolation Week Two

I'm down in the dumps
and I've got the grumps
'Cos my lifestyle has gone all astray.
It's hard to be cheerful
when I'm feeling tearful …
Can't stop myself feeling this way.

We're just two weeks in, but I'm only human
Like you and it's so hard to bear.
I know I am blessed
but by now you'll have guessed,
I'm fed up. I can't go anywhere.

BUT

I must pull up my socks
and take all the knocks
And work out just what I CAN do.
I'll devise a routine
with not too much cleaning
(Well maybe a hoover or two).

I can work out to apps, join the N.H.S. claps.
I can phone up a good friend or three.
I can dance to a tune. I can see the new moon.
I can even try doing Tai Chi.

I can sing. I can shout. I can wander about.
I can garden all day if I like.
I can eat all the sweets and give myself treats.
I can go on Geoff's exercise bike.

We're in difficult times
so I'll keep doing rhymes
'Cos I don't want to sit round and mope.
And I had an idea, then gave a big cheer
When I looked out my old skipping rope.

Don't know if I still can but I'll give it a try!

What Day Is It?

I wake up in the morning
and I feel rather dim!
Is it bridge today or shopping
or going for a swim?
No! None of these!
It's isolation in its umpteenth day.
I've lost all sense of date and time.
I think I've lost my way!

My breakfast's getting later
'cos I read my book in bed.
My lunch is getting earlier
'cos I plan it all ahead.
My evening drink's so tempting
that it's now at four o'clock.
Now, what time's supper?
Oh, I think I've got a mental block!

Bedtime's at ten o'clock these days.
It used to be eleven.
I think before this nightmare ends
I'll be in bed by SEVEN!

APRIL 2020

Our Future

How small I am. How insignificant.
One beating heart within a tiny space.
We are confined within ourselves,
our thoughts,
And yet we still make up the human race.
We are not free and yet the planet thrives.
Such harm we've done with selfish,
thoughtless lives.
The Earth is breathing,
blossoming in clean air.
The skies are full of stars. Life's everywhere!
Our world has shown us,
nature is our strength.
Will we take heed? Will we at last see sense?
How petty wars and prejudice seem to be
Faced with this threat to all humanity.
For we can see, we're BLESSED to be alive.
Without us all our planet STILL survives.

Stir Crazy (Or Am I Bored?)

Cheese on toast and beans on toast,
Eggs on toast, sardines on toast.
Never ending ways of eating toast!

THEN THERE'S

Marmalade and peanut butter,
Honey and Marmite too.
I always eat these upside down.
Don't you?

That's the toast upside down not me!

It Makes Sense

At first I was fighting
and longing and hoping.
I wondered however I'd live, but I'm coping!
I know I can do this. I know I'll survive
For all of my senses have now come alive.

I'm planning new menus
from store cupboard staples
Enjoying the taste of my food
And noticing texture and colour and smell
And the sound and the feel as it's chewed!

When I'm doing high kicks
along with Joe Wicks
I'm tasting each breath that I take.
I'm feeling it going right down to my lungs
And I'm hearing the sound that it makes.

Outside in the garden I'm being bombarded
With all the great flourish of spring.
The patterns in flowers. The touch of a leaf.
The robin puffed up when he sings.

The smell of the earth
as I sow my broad beans.
(And soon they'll be ready to eat!)
I'm seeing the ferns
tightly rolled at their cores
And the daisies abloom at my feet.

Touch, hear, taste and smell.
Notice details as well.
I'm happy to just simply BE.
Just try it and see. It's working for me
And I'm living my life in 5D!

MAY
2020

Topsy Turvey

My husband found a weed today
and shouted out with glee.
He waved it in the air
and then presented it to me!
We used to hate the weeding,
for everywhere they grew,
But now we find, with their persistence,
we've a job to do!

Today my sparkling window
had caught some pigeon poo.
How satisfying cleaning it again
as good as new.
And yesterday I spilt some milk
over the kitchen floor.
I was so happy mopping up,
I nearly spilt some more!

My world's gone topsy turvey
and chores I used to hate,
I welcome now with open arms,
even anticipate.
I'm seeing things with different eyes
and with a different view.
Perhaps that poor weed WANTS to grow
(and pigeons need to poo).

So when our world's turned right again,
you'll find a different me.
Considerate and tolerant,
that's what I'll try to be.

The Little Things

And now it's just the little things
that mean so much to me.
The birdsong through the window.
My morning cup of tea.
My breakfast's peanut butter,
spread thickly on my toast,
While Geoff enjoys the paper.
These things I value most.

And then we look for other things
to occupy our time.
Firstly we might phone a friend,
then I might pen a rhyme.
Then out into the garden,
it's bursting into bloom.
Our shed's become a summer house,
a lovely outdoor room.

The birdbath's filled with water.
A blackbird's splashing there,
The droplets falling all around.
We have to stand and stare.
We're noticing the details.
The first bud on the rose.
The tiny seedlings poking through.
The way the iris grows.

We're living in the moment.
We're GOING to get through.
We're trying to stay busy.
We're finding things to do.
One day we'll all be able to live
our lives again.

Time for another coffee …
Oh! It's only 5 to 10!

Time

The months are going quickly
but the days are oh so slow.
If it's already May then
where did March and April go?
My calendar is empty ...
it used to be so packed.
My future plans have all dissolved
and there's no going back.

I'm just existing in a void ...
no memories to make.
I'm busy doing useful things ...
I garden, clean and bake.
But where is the excitement,
the waiting for a treat,
The expectation, planning,
the daily meet and greet?

BUT

I must be more grateful
and appreciate this time.
I'm closer to my family with phone calls
and FaceTime.
My garden's blooming beautifully.
A walk is just sublime.
My home is clean and tidy
and I am feeling fine.

And there's a reason
for this glitch in all our daily lives.
It's so that we can save our world.
It's how we will survive.
We'll cut down all pollution,
recycle all our waste,
Be kinder and more tolerant,
to save the human race.
We'll cherish all the beauty
that surrounds us every day.
If there's a way to save the world
then we WILL find that way!

THANK YOU!

As I wake up to start the day,
I think what can I do?
Is there something to pass the time
and stop me feeling blue?
Today I looked around me
and suddenly I knew.
I'd spend my time appreciating and I'd say

THANK YOU!

Thank you for my family
and all the ones I love,
My lovely home so comfortable
it fits me like a glove
And my dear friends whose company
I once enjoyed so much
And for the new technology
that helps us keep in touch.

The list is never ending, for everywhere I see
The miracles of nature
and life surrounding me.
For food and drink, my life, my health,
I share this thought with you.
I'm richer than a millionaire
when I stop to say

THANK YOU!

I'm Only Human

Inside my head there's a place I dread.
I keep trying to close the door.
But the longer this lockdown
keeps rumbling on,
It's opening more and more.

It's full of despondence. It's full of despair.
It's full of concern for my family's welfare.
It's full of such longing to see them all soon,
To be with my friends,
for the world to resume,
For no global warming, no Covid 19.
It's full of depression. You see what I mean.

BUT

Inside my head there's a place I love.
I try to keep doors open wide
And the longer this shutdown
is staggering on
I NEED all the things there inside.

It's full of confidence. It's full of hope.
It's full of knowing that we will all cope.
It's valuing family. It's valuing friends.
It's confident this situation will end.
It's full of optimism, full of support,
Counting my blessings, positive thought.

When I keep the doors open
to this special place
You'll know that I'm there
by the smile on my face
And to make sure I'm accessing it
more and more,
The first has a padlock, this one
BIFOLD DOORS!

JUNE 2020

The Chelsea Pensioner

The sky was full of clouds today
with not a scrap of blue,
But suddenly they parted and the sun
came shining through.

And lockdown has been just like this,
some sunshine here and there.
A FaceTime with my family.
Phone calls to show we care.

The roses coming into bloom.
A stranger's smiling face.
A new walk or a special meal.
Enjoying our own space.

And then, today, on TV news,
a Chelsea Pensioner.
A twinkly, proud old gentleman
who smiled from ear to ear.

'I've got three meals a day,' he said.
'I sleep in my own bed
And best of all there's no one here
who wants to shoot me dead.'

And I respect that pensioner -
he knows how to survive.
Whatever happens now,
I too am glad to be ALIVE.

The Snail

The garden snail is not my friend.
He likes to eat my plants.
He glides around my seedlings
munching anything he wants.
And yes, he is intriguing
with his shell upon his back.
It's fascinating when his feelers
suddenly contract.
I like his shiny silver trail meandering along
But still I think my garden's not a place
where he belongs!

I sometimes think in life though,
that I'm a bit like him.
For there have been occasions
when I've drawn my feelers in.
I go along quite happily,
then suddenly a blow.
I want to hide inside my shell
while I find a way to go.

And when I'm getting really old,
I hope that I'll look back
And know that through my life
I'VE mostly left a silver track.

Joyce

30th JUNE 2020

Lifting

At last lockdown is lifting.
We're beginning to be free
To pick up threads of normal life
whilst going carefully.
And I can see my family
(with social distancing).
To just be in their company
means more than anything.
I can meet friends in the garden,
though we must stay apart.
It's wonderful to socialise again.
It lifts my heart.

For some it's been the worst of times,
for others not so bad,
But one thing's sure, we won't forget
the months that we've just had.
And many things have lifted me
and carried me along.
The constant of the N.H.S.
The beautiful birdsong.

The wonders of the garden,
the kindness, the support,
The FaceTime calls, the internet,
our shopping being brought.

And I have HOPE, it's lifting me,
the possibility
That we will share a greener world!
C19's legacy?

JULY 2020

Balance

I'm starting to feel wobbly.
Sometimes I veer off course.
My stout stick's helping me a lot
but I know it will get worse.
But LIVES are out of balance until C19 ends.
We're missing interaction -
seeing family and friends.
And some of us have too much work
and some of us have none.
And sometimes there is too much rain
and sometimes too much sun.

We're tired of isolation, of social distancing.
We're worried for our futures.
Will it be lose or win?
Yet nature's found its balance.
We've given it a rest
And in return it's flourished,
shown us its very best.

So when the whole world readjusts
and 'normal' life arrives,
I hope we'll all be lucky
and will all have balanced lives.

The Highland Cattle

The first time we walked
in the woods near Fleet
We knew we'd discovered
our special retreat.
Woods wrap you in peace.
There's barely a sound
As we follow the paths that meander around.

The trees help us breathe.
They've lived through the years
Withstanding this world
full of worries and fears.
The fall of a leaf. The whispering breeze.
It calms us to wander in places like these.

We've listened to birds and we saw a deer,
A doe with her fawn, standing so near,
As still as a statue but watching us pass
Then bowing to nibble upon the lush grass.

The greatest surprise we saw
through the trees,
A small herd of cattle, just wandering free.
They're huge Highland Cattle,
some with great curved horns.
So slow and so stately in this early morn.

We watched as the big male
just raised up his head
To enable two magpies
clear grubs from his bed.
Today he was scratching his neck
on some wood,
In a world of his own.
You could tell it felt good!

In sunshine or rain, when we come away,
We're glad that we walked there
at the start of our day.

Looking Up!

Do you ever take the time
to look up to the sky?
We're so busy living
and the days go quickly by.
But it is there ... eternally ... miraculously so.
It is a constant presence
in everything we know.

And it is all encompassing.
It makes me feel so small.
How sad we rarely notice
that it is there at all.
And every time that you look up
you'll have a unique view,
For no one else can see it
from the exact spot as you.

And all the time it will present
a view of endless change,
Perpetually moving ... familiar yet strange.

I look for shapes among the clouds
and it's a favourite game
And you can play it often
for the sky's never the same.

And I could write for hours
how the sky affects our mood.
A clear sky lifts our spirits.
The grey days make us brood.
Exciting on a breezy day,
unsettling in a storm
And breathtaking when sun
and rain create a rainbow's form.

And then there is the sky at night
with myriads of stars
And planets with their ancient names
like Jupiter and Mars.

I love to see the crescent moon ...
to me a sign of hope.
The full moon with its craters ...
I need a telescope!

My son has an experiment.
He calls it 'Daily View':
The garden changes gradually,
EACH DAY the sky is new!
I've made myself a promise
to look upward more each day
To wonder at the universe
as I go on my way.

7th JULY 2020

Captains Of Our Ships

The atmosphere's been stormy.
The seas have all been rough.
It's not all been plain sailing.
In fact it has been tough.
We've steered through many hazards
and faced long days at sea.
We've found the wind to fill our sails,
drunk endless cups of tea.
Good food's been cooked, we've cleaned
and baked. Much wine has passed our lips.
But in spite of all the challenges,
we're still CAPTAINS OF OUR SHIPS!

And now ahead, safe harbour.
Just steer around the rocks.
We'll come ashore to celebrate
when our ships are free to dock!

Masks

I used to smile at people
and pass the time of day,
But now it's most peculiar,
my mask gets in the way!
For when I look at people and
they look back at me
I can't tell how they're feeling.
I really just can't see.
I don't know if they want to talk
or simply walk on by.
It's very isolating
and it makes me shrug and sigh.
I find I'm in my bubble
keeping two metres apart.
Communication's disappeared.
Has everyone lost heart?

BUT

I'm lucky that I'm getting old
with wrinkles on my face,
For I have just discovered
that they're in a useful place!
For when I smile they gather
at the corners of my eyes
And you can SEE I'm smiling!

(I hope a nice surprise!)

AUGUST 2020

Reflections

We've got a garden table.
Its top is smokey glass
And when you look down into it,
you see the birds fly past!
While doing all the normal things
a table's meant to do
Its magical ingredient
is this breathtaking view.

The sky is just perfection,
so deep, the clouds so clear.
I marvel at the roses and anyone who's near.
It mirrors every detail.
It makes you look right in.
I could look down for hours
while contemplating things.

While I reflect upon my life,
the times that I've lived through,
My table makes me think
I'll take a different point of view.

Of course we've all had failures,
we've often made a mess,
But let's not dwell on our mistakes,
let's celebrate success!

It's no good looking backwards,
have complaints about our lot,
Let's just be glad that we are here,
enjoy the things we've got.
We owe it to our families.
We owe it to our friends,
To spread some fun and happiness
'til our existence ends.

Our table seats ten people,
or eight, or six, or four
(But mostly just the two of us
make up the daily score).

And even now, in lockdown,
we'll build happy memories
And our glass topped garden table
will be central in all these.

I hope we keep our table,
'cos now I'm old and grey
I remember all the happy times
I enjoyed along the way.

Strength

I saw a stunning picture,
a dried plant was centre stage.
It stood in all its glory, celebrating age.
Determined to keep straight and tall
and not hide in the shade,
Its structure and its character
defiantly displayed.

When age creeps up upon us,
although the bloom must fade,
We too should strive to face the world
and never be afraid.
We'll celebrate our wrinkles.
We'll plaster on a smile.
We'll show that life's not over yet
and go the extra mile.

For we have lived and should be proud
of all that we have done.
Let's not give up, ENJOY our lives
and look towards the sun.

The Dump

We'd make a collection of various things
and into the car we'd jump
And it became almost a weekly thing,
our regular trip to the dump.

There was always a queue
but we'd wait, as you do,
'til our turn came to empty our stuff.
BUT then came the day
when they turned us away
and we returned home in a huff!

We needed a slot
but there weren't a great lot
and I searched every day, but in vain.
There was never one free
and it wasn't just me,
all my friends said, 'It's really a pain.'

One evening at ten,
I tried once again.
There's a space there! Oh! Can it be free?
No matter what time,
that space will be mine!
Whatever the day, it's for ME!

So that morning at nine,
I waited in line,
(to be fair only one car ahead).
And dead on the dot,
I used up my slot,
then I phoned up my husband and said,

'This system is great.
You don't have to wait,
but we'll only come when there's a load.
It's very efficient,
each month is sufficient!'
and happily drove down the road.

Lockdown

It's now five months. Hard to believe
how much our lives have changed
And I can't dwell on things I miss
or I'd become deranged.
The only way I can survive
is living in each day
And celebrating things
that make a difference on the way.

Small things like the taste of beans and
beetroot that I've grown,
The smell of roses, flowers from the seeds
that I have sown
And relishing the raindrops
after weeks of lovely sun,
A good book and a glass of wine,
a puzzle that I've done.

Of course I have a routine,
but sometimes there's a treat
And now lockdown is lifting,
then some of us can meet.
It's magic seeing family,
although we still can't touch.
And sharing our experiences,
though we've not been doing much.

A walk with friends, a takeaway,
all stop me feeling bad
And it creates a highlight
I revisit when I'm sad.
But still, sometimes,
I just can't stop myself from feeling blue
And I'll be tired of doing things
that I'm allowed to do.

Are you like me?
When life is just not doing it for you,
Pick up the phone and call a friend
and help each other through.

My Cushion

One great thing about getting old
is many things I see
Ignite a spark within my head
which lights a memory.

Today I saw fritillaries and instantly recalled
My dad presenting some to mum ...
all snakey and piebald.
We'd never seen their like before ...
a special gift to bring.
I've loved them ever since.
They are a special part of spring.

My past's a great big cushion
no one can take away.
It's sometimes hard and sometimes soft
depending on my day!

A Cornish Pasty

Today I ate a pasty, a proper Cornish one
With pastry crimped along the sides
and steak to fill my tum.
And I remembered special times
in Padstow in the sun,
Sitting by the harbour wall,
laughing, having fun.

Then I remembered sticky toffeee apples
made by Mum
And sherbet dabs and liquorice sticks
and blowing bubble gum.
And chatting on the corner
after Youth Club eating chips,
Three pennorth wrapped in newspaper
with lots of crunchy bits.

And I could go right through my life
remembering great food,
Reliving special moments,
recapturing the mood.
I shared this thought with friends one day,
it brought smiles to our faces,
Recounting tales of favourite food
and happy times and places.

And now, in lockdown, on the days
when I am feeling bad,
I think of all the wonderful,
amazing food I've had
And as I relive all the times when
food has been involved,
I find that I've stopped feeling sad,
I'm smiling. Problem solved!

SEPTEMBER 2020

I Love Books!

I love to choose another book,
to read the opening page.
I know then whether I'll be bored
or if I'll be engaged.
Is there excitement waiting there?
A gripping story line?
Is it a book I can't put down
no matter what the time?

A book that will transport me
wholly to another world?
A book full of adventures
as the story is unfurled?
A book that will engross me?
Where I can lose myself?
Who knows what magic lies within
that book upon the shelf?

And I can read whilst travelling
by air or land or sea.
(It has to be a proper book,
ebooks are not for me.)
Whilst sunbathing on holiday …
while curled up by the fire,
Relaxing in the garden, a book's all I require.

And then to read in bed at night …
it switches off my brain
And stops my worries going round
and round and round again.
For as I read my bedtime book,
I soon begin to doze
And I know it's time to go to sleep
when my book falls on my nose!

Poohsticks

Sometimes on my daily walk
I cross a little brook.
Today there was a family there.
They'd stopped to take a look.
And they were playing Poohsticks
and having so much fun.
The little boy was scampering
to see if he had won!

It's always so exciting to see
which stick survives.
And we all know and love it.
We've played it all our lives.
It's being part of nature.
It's simple and it's fun.
(Though it's a bit embarrassing
when you're the only one!)

BUT

Today I have decided, next time
I'LL choose two sticks
And see which one's the fastest
And I'll DO it just for kicks!

Holding On!

On Thursday we got in the car
and went out for the day.
We travelled forty miles or more,
straight down the motorway.
It started raining heavily …
we kept on anyway,
But driving was quite difficult
with traffic causing spray.

At last we reached the forest
for a welcome cup of tea
But as I clambered from the car,
I called out 'Goodness me!'
For there upon the car's rear door,
a snail was clinging tight.
He'd travelled with us all the way.
He must have had a fright!

Through wind and rain, for many miles
he'd stayed inside his shell.
He must have wondered
what would happen to him if he fell.
So he'd just kept on holding on.
What a journey he'd been through.
BUT if a snail can do it, then we can do it too!

Keep holding on!

About The Author

Joyce has always enjoyed writing poems for family and friends but since reaching her 78th birthday she finds she has a whole new subject to write about ... how life feels when getting older and how she's trying to cope!

She wondered if anyone else would enjoy her rhymes and so started sharing them. As a result, Joyce discovered that her rhymes seemed to resonate and even sometimes help cheer her friends who in turn encouraged her to think about making them more widely available.

Joyce also has another book:
78 and Counting!

For up-to-date news, please visit
Joyce's website: www.78andcounting.com.

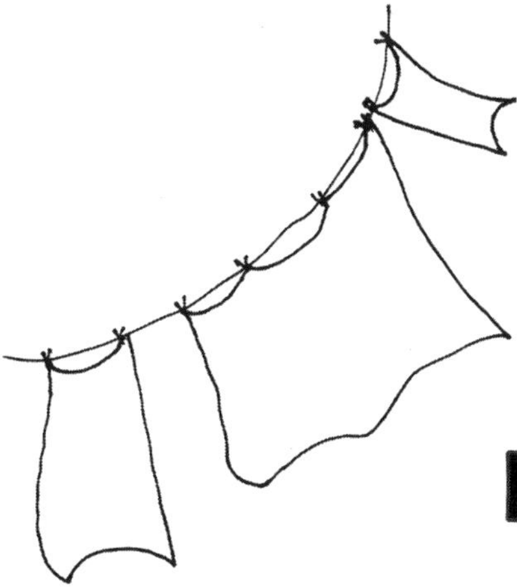

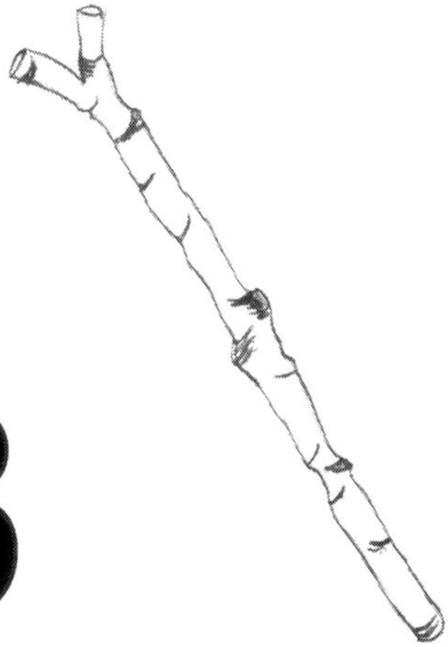

78 and Counting!

Joyce

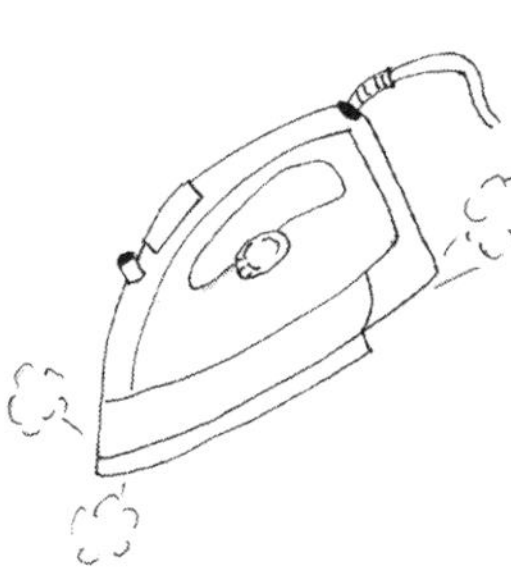